Thanksgiving Delights Journal

A Daily Journal

Hood Holiday Journal Series – Book 11

Karen Jean Matsko Hood

Thanksgiving Delights Journal

A Daily Journal
Hood Holiday Journal Series – Book 11

Gift Inscription

To: _____

From: _____

Date: _____

Special Message: _____

_____

_____

_____

_____

_____

_____

_____

It is always nice to receive a personal note to
create a special memory.

www.WhisperingPinePress.com
www.WhisperingPinePressBookstore.com

Thanksgiving Delights Journal

A Daily Journal

Hood Holiday Journal Series – Book 11

Karen Jean Matsko Hood

Published by:

Whispering Pine Press International, Inc.
Your Northwest Book Publishing Company
2510 North Pines Road, Suite 206, Sales Room
Spokane Valley, WA 99206-7636 USA
Phone: (509) 928-7888 | Fax: (509) 922-9949
Email: sales@whisperingpinepress.com
Websites: www.WhisperingPinePress.com
www.WhisperingPinePressBookstore.com
Blog: www.WhisperingPinePressBlog.com
SAN 253-200X
Printed in the U.S.A.

Published by Whispering Pine Press International, Inc.
International Publishing Company
2510 North Pines Road, Suite 206, Sales Room
Spokane Valley, WA 99206-7636 USA

For sales outside the United States, please contact the Whispering Pine Press International, Inc., International Sales Department.

Manufactured in the United States of America. This paper is acid-free and 100% chlorine free.

Book and Cover Design by Artistic Design Service, Inc.
Spokane Valley, WA 99206-7636 USA
www.ArtisticDesignService.com

Library of Congress Number (LCCN): 2014916769

Hood, Karen Jean Matsko
    Title: Thanksgiving Delights Journal: A Daily Journal, Hood Holiday Journal Series – Book 11

    p. cm.

ISBN: 978-1-59434-959-1   case bound
ISBN: 978-1-59434-960-7   perfect bound
ISBN: 978-1-59210-110-8   spiral bound
ISBN: 978-1-59210-111-5   E-PDF
ISBN: 978-1-59210-109-2   E-PUB
ISBN: 978-1-59434-168-7   E-PRC

First Edition: November 2014
1. Journal (*Thanksgiving Delights Journal: A Daily Journal, Hood Holiday Journal Series – Book 11*) 1. Title

Thanksgiving Delights Journal
A Daily Journal
Hood Holiday Journal Series – Book 11

Table of Contents

Did You Know? . . . .

Did you know that Plymouth Rock, the traditional site of disembarkation of William Bradford and the Mayflower Pilgrims, who founded Plymouth Colony, is described by some as "the most disappointing landmark in America" because of its small size and poor visitor access?

Did You Know? . . . .

Did you know that some who oppose consumerism have declared the day after Thanksgiving "Buy Nothing Day" in protest over that day being the beginning of the Christmas shopping season?

_____

_____

_____

_____

_____

_____

_____

_____

_____

_____

_____

_____

_____

_____

_____

_____

_____

Did You Know? . . . .

Did you know that since 2003 the public has been invited to vote on the names for the turkeys to be pardoned by the president?

_____

_____

_____

_____

_____

_____

_____

_____

_____

_____

_____

_____

_____

_____

_____

_____

_____

_____

Did You Know? . . . .

Did you know that the Macy's Thanksgiving Day Parade was suspended from 1942 to 1944 because the rubber and helium were needed for the World War II war effort?

_____
_____
_____
_____
_____
_____
_____
_____
_____
_____
_____
_____
_____
_____
_____
_____

Did You Know? . . . .

Did you know that wild turkeys while technically the same species as domesticated turkeys, have a very different taste from farm-raised turkeys? Almost all of the meat is "dark" (even the breasts) with a more intense turkey flavor. Older heritage breeds also differ in flavor.

_____

_____

_____

_____

_____

_____

_____

_____

_____

_____

_____

_____

_____

_____

_____

_____

_____

_____

14

Did You Know? . . . .

Did you know that Norman Rockwell featured a roast turkey as a symbol of prosperity in his painting "Freedom from Want"?

_____
_____
_____
_____
_____
_____
_____
_____
_____
_____
_____
_____
_____
_____
_____
_____
_____
_____
_____

Did You Know? . . . .

Did you know that the juice of red sweet potatoes is combined with lime juice to make a dye for cloth? By varying the proportions of the juices, every shade from pink to purple to black can be obtained.

_____
_____
_____
_____
_____
_____
_____
_____
_____
_____
_____
_____
_____
_____
_____
_____
_____

Did You Know? . . . .

Did you know that sweet potato leaves and shoots are a good source of vitamins A, C, and B2 (riboflavin)?

_____
_____
_____
_____
_____
_____
_____
_____
_____
_____
_____
_____
_____
_____
_____
_____
_____
_____
_____

Did You Know? . . . .

Did you know that today only about ⅓ of the top portion of Plymouth Rock remains? In its many journeys around Plymouth, numerous pieces of it were taken and bought and sold.

_____
_____
_____
_____
_____
_____
_____
_____
_____
_____
_____
_____
_____
_____
_____
_____
_____
_____

Did You Know? . . . .

Did you know that since 2005 the two turkeys pardoned by the president have been flown first class from Washington, D.C., to Los Angeles on United Airlines so they can be the Grand Marshals of Disneyland's annual Thanksgiving Day parade? They then live the rest of their lives at Disneyland's Frontierland ranch.

_____
_____
_____
_____
_____
_____
_____
_____
_____
_____
_____
_____
_____
_____
_____
_____

Did You Know? . . . .

Did you know that an attempt was made by Colonel Theophilus Cotton and the townspeople of Plymouth to move the Plymouth Rock in 1774? In the process the rock was split into two halves, and it was decided to leave the bottom portion behind at the wharf with the top half being relocated to the town's meetinghouse. In 1834 the upper portion of the Plymouth Rock was relocated from Plymouth's meetinghouse to Pilgrim Hall. Then in 1880, the top of the rock was moved from Pilgrim Hall back to its original wharf location and the date "1620" was carved into the rock.

Did You Know? . . . .

Did you know that in parts of Canada, pumpkin pie is commonly served with maple syrup instead of whipped cream?

_____
_____
_____
_____
_____
_____
_____
_____
_____
_____
_____
_____
_____
_____
_____
_____
_____
_____
_____

Did You Know? . . . .

Did you know that turkeys were a favorite domesticated animal among the Aztecs and were taken to Europe by the Spanish?

_____
_____
_____
_____
_____
_____
_____
_____
_____
_____
_____
_____
_____
_____
_____
_____
_____
_____

Did You Know? . . . .

Did you know that in 2004 the two turkeys pardoned by the President were named Biscuit and Gravy?

_____
_____
_____
_____
_____
_____
_____
_____
_____
_____
_____
_____
_____
_____
_____
_____
_____
_____
_____
_____

Did You Know? . . . .

Did you know that Samoset was the first Native American to make contact with the Pilgrims and that he brought Squanto a few days later because he spoke better English?

_____
_____
_____
_____
_____
_____
_____
_____
_____
_____
_____
_____
_____
_____
_____
_____

Did You Know? . . . .

Did you know that some animal welfare groups say that turkeys each have unique personalities and make wonderful companions?

_____

_____

_____

_____

_____

_____

_____

_____

_____

_____

_____

_____

_____

_____

_____

_____

Did You Know? . . . .

Did you know that in 2006 the two turkeys pardoned by the President were named Flyer and Fryer?

_____
_____
_____
_____
_____
_____
_____
_____
_____
_____
_____
_____
_____
_____
_____
_____
_____
_____

Did You Know? . . . .

Did you know that the world's biggest pumpkin pie weighed 418 pounds?

_____

_____

_____

_____

_____

_____

_____

_____

_____

_____

_____

_____

_____

_____

_____

_____

_____

Did You Know? . . . .

Did you know that when referring to balloons in parades, a falloon is a float-based balloon and a balloonicle is a self-powered balloon vehicle?

_____

_____

_____

_____

_____

_____

_____

_____

_____

_____

_____

_____

_____

_____

_____

_____

_____

Did You Know?....

Did you know that Tisquantum (Squanto) was kidnapped and taken to England, where he lived for nine years? He returned to the New World in 1913 with John Smith.

_____

_____

_____

_____

_____

_____

_____

_____

_____

_____

_____

_____

_____

_____

_____

Did You Know? . . . .

Did you know that Massachusetts is the second largest U.S. producer of cranberries, with over one-third of total domestic production?

_____
_____
_____
_____
_____
_____
_____
_____
_____
_____
_____
_____
_____
_____
_____
_____
_____
_____

Did You Know? . . . .

Did you know there are seven major varieties of sweet potatoes?

_____

_____

_____

_____

_____

_____

_____

_____

_____

_____

_____

_____

_____

_____

_____

_____

_____

_____

_____

Did You Know? . . . .

Did you know that the largest balloon to be in the Macy's parade was Superman?

_____
_____
_____
_____
_____
_____
_____
_____
_____
_____
_____
_____
_____
_____
_____

Did You Know? . . . .

Did you know that turkey is generally considered healthier and less fattening than red meat?

_____
_____
_____
_____
_____
_____
_____
_____
_____
_____
_____
_____
_____
_____
_____
_____
_____
_____
_____

Did You Know? . . . .

Did you know that a female domesticated turkey is called a hen, a chick is called a poult, and in the United States a male is called a tom, but in Europe a male is called a stag?

_____

_____

_____

_____

_____

_____

_____

_____

_____

_____

_____

_____

_____

_____

_____

_____

_____

Did You Know? . . . .

Did you know that turkey droppings are planned to fuel an electric power plant in western Minnesota that will begin operating in 2007? The plant will provide 55 megawatts of power using 700,000 tons of dung per year. Three such plants are in operation in England.

_____

_____

_____

_____

_____

_____

_____

_____

_____

_____

_____

_____

_____

_____

_____

_____

_____

_____

_____

_____

Did You Know? . . . .

Did you know that 1941 was the year Congress passed a joint resolution that set Thanksgiving on the fourth Thursday of November, where it remains today?

_____

_____

_____

_____

_____

_____

_____

_____

_____

_____

_____

_____

_____

_____

_____

_____

_____

_____

_____

_____

_____

59

Did You Know? . . . .

Did you know that the average lifespan for a turkey is 10 years?

_____
_____
_____
_____
_____
_____
_____
_____
_____
_____
_____
_____
_____
_____
_____
_____
_____
_____
_____

Did You Know? . . . .

Did you know that in Mexico, turkey meat with mole sauce is widely regarded as the unofficial national dish?

_____
_____
_____
_____
_____
_____
_____
_____
_____
_____
_____
_____
_____
_____
_____
_____
_____
_____

Did You Know? . . . .

Did you know that fresh cranberries can be frozen at home and will keep up to nine months? They can be used directly in recipes without thawing.

_____
_____
_____
_____
_____
_____
_____
_____
_____
_____
_____
_____
_____
_____
_____
_____
_____
_____

Did You Know? . . . .

Did you know that the young leaves and vine tips of sweet potatoes are widely consumed as a vegetable in some West African countries?

_____
_____
_____
_____
_____
_____
_____
_____
_____
_____
_____
_____
_____
_____
_____
_____
_____
_____
_____

Did you know that in the Midwestern United States in the mid to late 1800s, domestic turkeys were actually herded across the range in a manner similar to herding cattle?

_____

_____

_____

_____

_____

_____

_____

_____

_____

_____

_____

_____

_____

_____

_____

_____

_____

_____

Did You Know? . . . .

Did you know that in the Middle Ages stuffing was known as farce, from the Latin farcire, which means to stuff? The term "stuffing" first appears in English print in 1538. After about 1880, the term "stuffing" was replaced by "dressing" in Victorian English.

_____

_____

_____

_____

_____

_____

_____

_____

_____

_____

_____

_____

_____

_____

_____

_____

_____

_____

Did You Know?....

Did you know that gourds are from the same family as squashes?

_____
_____
_____
_____
_____
_____
_____
_____
_____
_____
_____
_____
_____
_____
_____
_____
_____
_____

Did You Know?....

Did you know that American Revolutionary War veteran Henry Hall is alleged to be the first to cultivate the cranberry commercially around 1816?

_____
_____
_____
_____
_____
_____
_____
_____
_____
_____
_____
_____
_____
_____
_____
_____
_____
_____

Did You Know? . . . .

Did you know that cranberries are a major commercial crop in certain U.S. states and Canadian provinces?

_____
_____
_____
_____
_____
_____
_____
_____
_____
_____
_____
_____
_____
_____
_____
_____
_____
_____

Did You Know? . . . .

Did you know that Wisconsin is the leading producer of cranberries, with nearly half of U.S. production?

_____
_____
_____
_____
_____
_____
_____
_____
_____
_____
_____
_____
_____
_____
_____
_____
_____

Did You Know? . . . .

Did you know that in 2003 the two turkeys pardoned by the President were named Stars and Stripes?

_____
_____
_____
_____
_____
_____
_____
_____
_____
_____
_____
_____
_____
_____
_____
_____
_____
_____

Did You Know? . . . .

Did you know that when eaten at Christmas in Britain, turkey is traditionally served with winter vegetables, including roast potatoes, Brussels sprouts, and parsnips?

_____

_____

_____

_____

_____

_____

_____

_____

_____

_____

_____

_____

_____

_____

_____

_____

_____

Did You Know? . . . .

Did you know that in North America, Native Americans were the first to recognize and use the cranberry as a source of food?

_____
_____
_____
_____
_____
_____
_____
_____
_____
_____
_____
_____
_____
_____
_____
_____
_____
_____

Did You Know? . . . .

Did you know that about 95 percent of cranberries are processed into products such as juice drinks, sauce, and sweetened dried cranberries? The remaining 5 percent are sold fresh to consumers.

_____
_____
_____
_____
_____
_____
_____
_____
_____
_____
_____
_____
_____
_____
_____
_____

Did You Know? . . . .

Did you know that 1934 was the first year a Mickey Mouse balloon was entered in the Macy's Thanksgiving Day Parade?

_____

_____

_____

_____

_____

_____

_____

_____

_____

_____

_____

_____

_____

_____

_____

_____

_____

_____

_____

Did You Know? . . . .

Did you know that a child born at sea on the Mayflower was named Oceanus?

_____
_____
_____
_____
_____
_____
_____
_____
_____
_____
_____
_____
_____
_____
_____
_____
_____
_____

Did You Know? . . . .

Did you know that according to the USDA, one-sixth of the more than 45 million turkeys that are sold in the U.S. each year are cooked and eaten for Thanksgiving?

_____

_____

_____

_____

_____

_____

_____

_____

_____

_____

_____

_____

_____

_____

_____

_____

_____

_____

_____

Did You Know? . . . .

Did you know that in 2005 the two turkeys pardoned by the President were named Marshmallow and Yam?

_____

_____

_____

_____

_____

_____

_____

_____

_____

_____

_____

_____

_____

_____

_____

_____

_____

Did You Know? . . . .

Did you know that there is no evidence to support the claim that turkey was served at the first Thanksgiving?

_____
_____
_____
_____
_____
_____
_____
_____
_____
_____
_____
_____
_____
_____
_____
_____
_____

Did You Know? . . . .

Did you know that birds and other pests which usually flock to fruit crops leave cranberries alone?

_____
_____
_____
_____
_____
_____
_____
_____
_____
_____
_____
_____
_____
_____
_____
_____

Did You Know? . . . .

Did you know that cranberries can be grown almost anywhere in your garden where the soil is acidic?

_____
_____
_____
_____
_____
_____
_____
_____
_____
_____
_____
_____
_____
_____
_____
_____
_____
_____

Did You Know? . . . .

Did you know that pumpkins and winter squash can be harvested whenever they are a deep, solid color and the rind is hard?

_____
_____
_____
_____
_____
_____
_____
_____
_____
_____
_____
_____
_____
_____
_____
_____

Did You Know? . . . .

   Did you know that other dishes associated with the Thanksgiving meal are stuffing, mashed potatoes and gravy, sweet potatoes, cranberry sauce, corn, and pumpkin pie?

_____
_____
_____
_____
_____
_____
_____
_____
_____
_____
_____
_____
_____
_____
_____
_____
_____
_____

Did You Know? . . . .

Did you know that in New York City, the Macy's Thanksgiving Day Parade is held annually every Thanksgiving Day?

_____
_____
_____
_____
_____
_____
_____
_____
_____
_____
_____
_____
_____
_____
_____
_____
_____
_____
_____

Did You Know? . . . .

Did you know that according to legend, Ben Franklin thought the North American wild turkey should be the national bird?

_____
_____
_____
_____
_____
_____
_____
_____
_____
_____
_____
_____
_____
_____
_____
_____
_____

Did You Know? . . . .

Did you know that the idea of the Thanksgiving feast is to eat more than you can possibly eat? You have to eat until you are groaning.

_____
_____
_____
_____
_____
_____
_____
_____
_____
_____
_____
_____
_____
_____
_____
_____
_____

Did You Know? . . . .

Did you know that the story of Thanksgiving is basically the story of the Pilgrims and their thankful community feast at Plymouth, Massachusetts?

_____

_____

_____

_____

_____

_____

_____

_____

_____

_____

_____

_____

_____

_____

_____

_____

_____

Did You Know? . . . .

Did you know that Thanksgiving was proclaimed by every president after Lincoln? The date was changed a few times.

_____
_____
_____
_____
_____
_____
_____
_____
_____
_____
_____
_____
_____
_____
_____
_____
_____

Did You Know? . . . .

Did you know that if growing cranberries in a hanging basket, watch out for the critical period in September and early October when it is easy to relax and pay less attention to watering?

_____
_____
_____
_____
_____
_____
_____
_____
_____
_____
_____
_____
_____
_____
_____
_____
_____

Did You Know? . . . .

Did you know that pumpkins and winter squash are very tender vegetables?

_____
_____
_____
_____
_____
_____
_____
_____
_____
_____
_____
_____
_____
_____
_____
_____
_____
_____

Did You Know? . . . .

Did you know that sweet potatoes are started from plants called "slips?" Transplant slips as soon as soil warms up after the last frost.

_____
_____
_____
_____
_____
_____
_____
_____
_____
_____
_____
_____
_____
_____
_____
_____

Did You Know? . . . .

Did you know that in the float that traditionally ends the Macy's Parade is the Santa Claus float?

_____
_____
_____
_____
_____
_____
_____
_____
_____
_____
_____
_____
_____
_____
_____

Did You Know? . . . .

Did you know that the timing of Thanksgiving—at the point in the fall season when the traditional harvesting is completed—also contributes to its symbolic power?

_____

_____

_____

_____

_____

_____

_____

_____

_____

_____

_____

_____

_____

_____

_____

_____

_____

Did You Know? . . . .

Did you know that George Washington was the first president to declare Thanksgiving a holiday, in 1789?

_____
_____
_____
_____
_____
_____
_____
_____
_____
_____
_____
_____
_____
_____
_____
_____
_____

Did You Know? . . . .

Did you know that the sweet potato has been used as a food source since before recorded history?

_____
_____
_____
_____
_____
_____
_____
_____
_____
_____
_____
_____
_____
_____
_____
_____
_____

Did You Know? . . . .

Did you know that the Mayflower was a small ship crowded with men, women, and children, besides the sailors on board?

_____
_____
_____
_____
_____
_____
_____
_____
_____
_____
_____
_____
_____
_____
_____
_____

Did You Know? . . . .

Did you know that the first such Thanksgiving, as the Pilgrims would have called it, did not occur until 1623, in response to the good news of the arrival of additional colonists and supplies?

_____
_____
_____
_____
_____
_____
_____
_____
_____
_____
_____
_____
_____
_____
_____
_____
_____

Did You Know? . . . .

Did you know that the orange flesh of the pumpkin is a dead giveaway that it is a source of beta carotene, which is a powerful antioxidant?

_____

_____

_____

_____

_____

_____

_____

_____

_____

_____

_____

_____

_____

_____

_____

_____

_____

_____

Did You Know? . . . .

Did you know that compared with other meats, turkey has fewer calories, less fat, less cholesterol, and very little sodium, but it is high in protein, vitamins, and minerals?

_____
_____
_____
_____
_____
_____
_____
_____
_____
_____
_____
_____
_____
_____
_____
_____
_____

Did You Know? . . . .

    Did you know that cranberry bogs in America, where cranberries are commercially grown, are deliberately flooded to make harvesting easier?

_____
_____
_____
_____
_____
_____
_____
_____
_____
_____
_____
_____
_____
_____
_____
_____
_____

Did You Know? . . . .

Did you know that most of the fat in turkey is within the skin, and most of the fat within the meat is in the dark meat?

_____
_____
_____
_____
_____
_____
_____
_____
_____
_____
_____
_____
_____
_____
_____
_____
_____

Did You Know? . . . .

Did you know that turkey is an excellent source of several important vitamins and nutrients such as iron, niacin, zinc, potassium, and B vitamins?

_____

_____

_____

_____

_____

_____

_____

_____

_____

_____

_____

_____

_____

_____

_____

_____

Did You Know? . . . .

Did you know that the white meat with the skin removed is a good food source for people on low-fat and/or low sodium diets? The meat fiber is easier to digest than other types of meat, which makes it a good choice for individuals who may have digestive problems?

_____
_____
_____
_____
_____
_____
_____
_____
_____
_____
_____
_____
_____
_____
_____
_____

Dedications

To my husband and best friend, Jim.

To our seventeen children: Gabriel, Brianne Kristina and her husband Moulik Vinodkumar Kothari, Marissa Kimberly and her husband Kevin Matthew Franck, Janelle Karina and her husband Paul Joseph Turcotte, Mikayla Karlene, Kyler James, Kelsey Katrina, Corbin Joel, Caleb Jerome, Keisha Kalani Hiwot, Devontay Joshua, Kianna Karielle Selam, Rosy Kiara, Mercedes Katherine, Jasmine Khalia Wengel, Cheyenne Krystal, and Annalise Kaylee Marie.

To Nola Paige, Zoey Karina, and future grandchildren.

To our foster grandchildren: Courtney, Lorenzo, and Leah.

To my brother, Stephen, and his wife, Karen.

To my husband's ten siblings: Gary, Colleen, John, Dan, Mary, Ray, Ann, Teresa, Barbara, Agnes, and their families.

In loving memory of my mom, who passed away in 2007; my dad, who passed away in 1976; and my sister, Sandy, who passed away due to multiple sclerosis in 1999.

To Sandy's three sons: Monte, Bradley, and Derek. To Monte's wife, Sarah, and their children: Liam, Alice, Charlie, Samuel and their foster children. To Bradley's wife, Shawnda, and their children: Anton, Isaac, and Isabel.

To our foster children past and present: Krystal, Sara, Rebecca, Janice, Devontay Joshua, Mercedes Katherine, Zha'Nell, Makia, Onna, Cheyenne Krystal, Onna Marie, Nevaeh, and Zada, our future foster children, and all foster children everywhere.

To the Court Appointed Special Advocate (CASA) Volunteer Program in the judicial system which benefits abused and neglected children.

To the Literacy Campaign dedicated to promoting literacy throughout the world.

Acknowledgements

The author would like to acknowledge all those individuals who helped me during my time in writing this book. Appreciation is extended for all their support and effort they put into this project.

Deep gratitude and profound thanks are owed to my husband, Jim, for giving freely of his time and encouragement during this project.

Also, thanks are owed to my children Gabriel, Brianne Kristina and her husband Moulik Vinodkumar Kothari, Marissa Kimberly and her husband Kevin Matthew Franck, Janelle Karina and her husband Paul Joseph Turcotte, Mikayla Karlene, Kyler James, Kelsey Katrina, Corbin Joel, Caleb Jerome, Keisha Kalani Hiwot, Devontay Joshua, Kianna Karielle Selam, Rosy Kiara, Mercedes Katherine, Jasmine Khalia Wengel, Cheyenne Krystal, and Annalise Kaylee Marie. All of these persons inspire my writing.

Thanks are due to Pam Alexandrovich and Sharron Thompson for their assistance in editing and typing this manuscript for publication. Thanks go to Artistic Design Service, Inc. for their assistance in formatting and providing a graphic design of this manuscript for publication. This project could not have been completed without them.

Many thanks are due to members of my family, all of whom were very supportive during the time it took to complete this project. Their patience and support are greatly appreciated.

Praise for Thanksgiving Delights Journal
A Daily Journal
Hood Holiday Journal Series – Book 11

…"Each year I like to search for fun, new, and creative ways to surprise my family on Thanksgiving Day. Since discovering *Thanksgiving Delights Journal*, I've been able to record my memories.

There are many ideas in this journal to help you show your children and friends just how much they mean to you. Treat yourself or someone you love to a copy of this journal today!"…

Kimberly Carter
Assistant

…"*Thanksgiving Delights Journal* has blank pages for you to write your own notes or recipes.

Thanksgiving Delights Journal will soon be part of your treasured collection of splendid holiday records to be passed down to future generations."…

Mary Scripture-Smith
Graphic Designer

Praise for Thanksgiving Delights Journal
A Daily Journal
Hood Holiday Journal Series - Book 11

…"Whispering Pine Press International has done it again with the newest in their Cookbook Delights Holiday Series collection. *Thanksgiving Delights Journal* continues the legacy of high quality work and craftsmanship from its author. The journal pages are designed to leave space to write your own journal notes and favorite recipes."…

Allyson Schnabel
Editor, Teacher

…"*Thanksgiving Delights Journal* is a companion to Thanksgiving Delights Cookbook. It gives you space to write your own journal notes or your favorite recipes."…

Ed Archambeault
Spokane, WA.

Reader Feedback Form

Dear Reader,

We are very interested in what our readers think. Please fill in the form below and return to:

Whispering Pine Press International, Inc.
c/o Thanksgiving Delights Journal: A Daily Journal
2510 North Pines Road, Suite 206, Sales Room
Spokane Valley, WA 99206-7636 USA
Phone: (509) 928-7888 | Fax: (509) 922-9949
Email: sales@whisperingpinepress.com
Publisher Websites: www.WhisperingPinePress.com
www.WhisperingPinePressBookstore.com
Blog: www.WhisperingPinePressBlog.com

Name: _____

Address: _____

City, St., Zip: _____

Phone/Fax: (____) _____ | (____) _____

Email: _____

Comments/Suggestions: _____

_____

_____

_____

_____

A great deal of care and attention has been exercised in the creation of this book. Designing a great cookbook that is original, fun, and easy to use has been a job that required many hours of diligence, creativity, and research. Although we strive to make this book completely error free, errors and discrepancies may not be completely excluded. If you come across any errors or discrepancies, please make a note of them and send them to our publishing office. We are constantly updating our manuscripts, eliminating errors, and improving quality.

Please contact us at the address above.

About the Cookbook Delights Series

The *Cookbook Delights Series* includes many different topics and themes. If you have a passion for food and wish to know more information about different foods, then this series of cookbooks will be beneficial to you. Each book features a different type of food, such as avocados, strawberries, huckleberries, salmon, vegetarian, lentils, almonds, cherries, coconuts, lemons, and many, many more.

The *Cookbook Delights Series* not only includes cookbooks about individual foods but also includes several holiday-themed cookbooks. Whatever your favorite holiday may be, chances are we have a cookbook with recipes designed with that holiday in mind. Some examples include *Halloween Delights, Thanksgiving Delights, Christmas Delights, Valentine Delights, Mother's Day Delights, St. Patrick's Day Delights,* and *Easter Delights.*

Each cookbook is designed for easy use and is organized into alphabetical sections. Over 250 recipes are included along with other interesting facts, folklore, and history of the featured food or theme. Each book comes with a beautiful full-color cover, ordering information, and a list of other upcoming books in the series.

Note cards, bookmarks, and a daily journal have been printed and are available to go along with each cookbook. You may view the entire line of cookbooks, journals, cards, posters, puzzles, and bookmarks by visiting our website at www.whisperingpinepress. com, or you can email us with your questions and your comments to: sales@whisperingpinepress.com.

Please ask your local bookstore to carry these sets of books.

To order, please contact:

Whispering Pine Press International, Inc.
c/o Thanksgiving Delights Journal: A Daily Journal
2510 North Pines Road, Suite 206, Sales Room
Spokane Valley, WA 99206-7636 USA
Phone: (509) 928-7888 | Fax: (509) 922-9949
Email: sales@whisperingpinepress.com
Publisher Websites: www.WhisperingPinePress.com
www.WhisperingPinePressBookstore.com
Blog: www.WhisperingPinePressBlog.com
SAN 253-200X

We Invite You to Join the Whispering Pine Press International, Inc. Book Club!

Whispering Pine Press International, Inc.
c/o Thanksgiving Delights Journal: A Daily Journal
2510 North Pines Road, Suite 206, Sales Room
Spokane Valley, WA 99206-7636 USA
Phone: (509) 928-7888 | Fax: (509) 922-9949
Email: sales@whisperingpinepress.com
Publisher Websites: www.WhisperingPinePress.com
www.WhisperingPinePressBookstore.com
Blog: www.WhisperingPinePressBlog.com

Buy 11 books and get the next one free, based on the average price of the first eleven purchased.

How the club works:

Simply use the order form below and order books from our catalog. You can buy just one at a time or all eleven at once. After the first eleven books are purchased, the next one is free. Please add shipping and handling as listed on this form. There are no purchase requirements at any time during your membership. Free book credit is based on the average price of the first eleven books purchased.

Join today! Pick your books and mail in the form today!

Yes! I want to join the Whispering Pine Press International, Inc., Book Club! Enroll me and send the books indicated below.

Title   Price

1. _____

2. _____

3. _____

4. _____

5. _____

6. _____

7. _____

8. _____

9. _____

10. _____

11. _____

Free Book Title: _____

Free Book Price: _____ Avg. Price: _____ Total Price: _____

Credit for the free book is based on the average price of the first 11 books purchased.

(Circle one) Check | Visa | MasterCard | Discover | American Express

Credit Card #: _____ Expiration Date: _____

Name: _____

Address: _____

City: _____ State: _____ Country: _____

Zip/Postal: _____ Phone: (_____) _____

Email: _____

Signature_____

Whispering Pine Press International, Inc.
Fundraising Opportunities

Fundraising cookbooks are proven moneymakers and great keepsake providers for your group. Whispering Pine Press International, Inc., offers a very special personalized cookbook fundraising program that encourages success to organizations all across the USA.

Our prices are competitive and fair. Currently, we offer a special of 100 books with many free features and excellent customer service. Any purchase you make is guaranteed first-rate.

Flexibility is not a problem. If you have special needs, we guarantee our cooperation in meeting each of them. Our goal is to create a cookbook that goes beyond your expectations. We have the confidence and a record that promises continual success.

Another great fundraising program is the *Cookbook Delights Series* Program. With cookbook orders of 50 copies or more, your organization receives a huge discount, making for a prompt and lucrative solution.

We also specialize in assisting group fundraising – Christian, community, nonprofit, and academic among them. If you are struggling for a new idea, something that will enhance your success and broaden your appeal, Whispering Pine Press International, Inc., can help.

For more information, write, phone, or fax to:

Whispering Pine Press International, Inc.
2510 North Pines Road, Suite 206, Sales Room
Spokane Valley, WA 99206-7636 USA
Phone: (509) 928-7888 | Fax: (509) 922-9949
Email: sales@whisperingpinepress.com
Publisher Websites: www.WhisperingPinePress.com
www.WhisperingPinePressBookstore.com
Blog: www.WhisperingPinePressBlog.com
SAN 253-200X

Personalized and/or Translated Order Form for Any Book by Whispering Pine Press International, Inc.

Dear Readers:

If you or your organization wishes to have this book or any other of our books personalized, we will gladly accommodate your needs. For instance, if you would like to change the names of the characters in a book to the names of the children in your family or Sunday school class, we would be happy to work with you on such a project. We can add more information of your choosing and customize this book especially for your family, group, or organization.

We are also offering an option of translating your book into another language. Please fill out the form below telling us exactly how you would like us to personalize your book.

Please send your request to:

Whispering Pine Press International, Inc.
c/o Thanksgiving Delights Journal: A Daily Journal
2510 North Pines Road, Suite 206, Sales Room
Spokane Valley, WA 99206-7636 USA
Phone: (509) 928-7888 | Fax: (509) 922-9949
Email: sales@whisperingpinepress.com
Publisher Websites: www.WhisperingPinePress.com
www.WhisperingPinePressBookstore.com
Blog: www.WhisperingPinePressBlog.com

Person/Organization placing request: _____
_____Date: _____
Phone: (____) _____ Fax: (____) _____
Address: _____
City: _____ State: _____ Zip: _____
Language of the book: _____
Please explain your request in detail: _____
_____
_____
_____
_____

Thanksgiving Delights Journal
A Daily Journal
Hood Holiday Journal Series – Book 11
How to Order

Get your additional copies of this book by returning an order form and your check, money order, or credit card information to:

Whispering Pine Press International, Inc.
c/o Thanksgiving Delights Journal: A Daily Journal
2510 North Pines Road, Suite 206, Sales Room
Spokane Valley, WA 99206-7636 USA
Phone: (509) 928-7888 | Fax: (509) 922-9949
Email: sales@whisperingpinepress.com
Publisher Websites: www.WhisperingPinePress.com
www.WhisperingPinePressBookstore.com
Blog: www.WhisperingPinePressBlog.com

Customer Name: _____

Address: _____

City, St., Zip: _____

Phone/Fax: _____

Email: _____

- -

Please send me _____ copies of _____ _____

_____ at $_____ per copy and $5.95 for

shipping and handling per book, plus $3.95 each for additional books. Enclosed

is my check, money order, or charge my account for $_____.

☐ Check ☐ Money Order ☐ Credit Card

(*Circle One*) MasterCard | Discover | Visa | American Express
☐☐☐☐ ☐☐☐☐ ☐☐☐☐ ☐☐☐☐

Expiration Date: _____

_____
Signature

_____
Print Name

Whispering Pine Press International, Inc. Order Form
Gift-wrapping, Autographing, and Inscription
We are proud to offer personal autographing by the author. For a limited time this service is absolutely free!
Gift-wrapping is also available for $4.95 per item.

1. Sold To
Name: _____
Street/Route: _____

_____
City: _____
State: _____ Zip: _____
Country: _____
Gift message: _____

_____
Email address: _____
Daytime Phone: (＿＿) ＿＿＿-＿＿＿＿
*Necessary for verifying orders
Home Phone: (＿＿) ＿＿＿-＿＿＿＿
Fax: (＿＿) ＿＿＿-＿＿＿＿

2. Ship To
☐ Is this a new or corrected address?

☐ Alternative Shipping Address

☐ Mailing Address
Name: _____
Address: _____

_____
City: _____
State: _____ Zip: _____
Country: _____
Email address: _____

3. Items Ordered

ISBN # /Item #	Size	Color	Qty.	Title or Description	Price	Total

4. Method Of Payment
International, Inc. (No Cash or COD's)

☐ Visa ☐ MasterCard ☐ Discover ☐ American Express ☐ Check/Money Order
Please make it payable to Whispering Pine Press International, Inc. (No Cash or COD's)

Account Number   Expiration Date
                        _____ / _____
                         Month Year

☐☐☐☐ ☐☐☐☐ ☐☐☐☐ ☐☐☐☐

Signature_____
          Cardholder's signature
Printed Name_____
          Please print name of cardholder
Address of Cardholder_____

Subtotal	
Gift wrap $4.95 Each	
For delivery in WA add 8.7% sales tax.	
Shipping See chart at left	
6. Total	

5. Shipping & Handling

Continental US
US Postal Ground: For books please add $4.95 for the first book and $2.95 each for additional books.
All non-book items, add 15% of the Subtotal.
Please allow 1-4 weeks for delivery.
US Postal Air: Please add $15.00 shipping and handling.
Please allow 1-3 days for delivery.
Alaska, Hawaii, and the US Territories By Ship:
Please add 10% shipping and handling
(minimum charge $15.00).

Please
By Air: Please add 12% shipping and handling (minimum charge $15.00).
Please allow 2 –6 weeks for delivery.
International By Ship: Please add 10% shipping and handling (minimum charge $15.00).
Please allow 6-12 weeks for delivery.
By Air: Please add 12% shipping and handling (minimum charge $15.00).
Please allow 2-6 weeks for delivery.
FedEx Shipments: Add $5.00 to the above airmail charges for overnight delivery.

Shop Online:
www.WhisperingPinePress.com
Fax orders to: (509) 922-9949

Whispering Pine Press International, Inc.
2510 North Pines Road, Suite 206, Sales Room
Spokane Valley, WA 99206-7636 USA
Phone: (509) 928-7888 • Fax: (509) 922-9949
Email: sales@whisperingpinepress.com
Website: www.WhisperingPinePress.com

Whispering Pine Press International, Inc. Order Form

Gift-wrapping, Autographing, and Inscription

We are proud to offer personal autographing by the author. For a limited time this service is absolutely free!
Gift-wrapping is also available for $4.95 per item.

1. Sold To

Name: _____
Street/Route: _____

_____
City: _____
State: _____ Zip: _____
Country: _____
Gift message: _____

_____
Email address: _____
Daytime Phone: (_ _ _) _ _ _ - _ _ _ _
*Necessary for verifying orders
Home Phone: (_ _ _) _ _ _ - _ _ _ _
Fax: (_ _ _) _ _ _ - _ _ _ _

2. Ship To

☐ Is this a new or corrected address?

☐ Alternative Shipping Address

☐ Mailing Address

Name: _____
Address: _____

_____
City: _____
State: _____ Zip: _____
Country: _____
Email address: _____

3. Items Ordered

ISBN # /Item #	Size	Color	Qty.	Title or Description	Price	Total

4. Method Of Payment

International, Inc. (No Cash or COD's)

☐ Visa ☐ MasterCard ☐ Discover ☐ American Express ☐ Check/Money Order

Please make it payable to Whispering Pine Press International, Inc. (No Cash or COD's)

Account Number   Expiration Date
                        _____ / _____
                        Month Year

☐☐☐☐ ☐☐☐☐ ☐☐☐☐ ☐☐☐☐

Signature_____
        Cardholder's signature
Printed Name_____
        Please print name of cardholder
Address of Cardholder_____

Subtotal	
Gift wrap $4.95 Each	
For delivery in WA add 8.7% sales tax.	
Shipping See chart at left	
6. Total	

5. Shipping & Handling

Continental US

US Postal Ground: For books please add $4.95 for the first book and $2.95 each for additional books.
All non-book items, add 15% of the Subtotal.
Please allow 1-4 weeks for delivery.
US Postal Air: Please add $15.00 shipping and handling.
Please allow 1-3 days for delivery.
Alaska, Hawaii, and the US Territories By Ship:
Please add 10% shipping and handling
(minimum charge $15.00).

Please
By Air: Please add 12% shipping and handling (minimum charge $15.00).
Please allow 2 –6 weeks for delivery.
International By Ship: Please add 10% shipping and handling (minimum charge $15.00).
Please allow 6-12 weeks for delivery.
By Air: Please add 12% shipping and handling (minimum charge $15.00).
Please allow 2-6 weeks for delivery.
FedEx Shipments: Add $5.00 to the above airmail charges for overnight delivery.

Shop Online:
www.WhisperingPinePress.com
Fax orders to: (509) 922-9949

Whispering Pine Press International, Inc.
2510 North Pines Road, Suite 206, Sales Room
Spokane Valley, WA 99206-7636 USA
Phone: (509) 928-7888 • Fax: (509) 922-9949
Email: sales@whisperingpinepress.com
Website: www.WhisperingPinePress.com

CURRENT AND FUTURE BOOKS FOR ADULTS
by Karen Jean Matsko Hood

Hood Holiday Journal Series

New Years Delights Journal –
  Book 1
Valentine Delights Journal –
  Book 2
St. Patrick's Day Delights
  Journal – Book 3
Easter Delights Journal – Book 4
Mother's Day Delights Journal –
  Book 5
Memorial Day Delights Journal –
  Book 6
Father's Day Delights Journal –
  Book 7
Fourth of July Delights Journal –
  Book 8
Labor Day Delights Journal –
  Book 9
Halloween Delights Journal –
  Book 10
Thanksgiving Delights Journal –
  Book 11
Christmas Delights Journal –
  Book 12

Hood Journal Series

Apple Delights Journal – Book 1
Blueberry Delights – Book 2
Chocolate Delights Journal – Book 3
Grape Delights Journal – Book 4
Huckleberry Delights Journal – Book 5
Lentil Delights Journal – Book 6
Onion Delights Journal – Book 7
Peach Delights Journal – Book 8
Pear Delights Journal – Book 9
Plum Delights Journal – Book 10
Prickly Pear Delights Journal – Book 11
Pumpkin Delights Journal – Book 12
Raspberry Delights Journal – Book 13
Rhubarb Delights Journal – Book 14
Strawberry Delights Journal – Book 15
Tea Time Delights Journal – Book 16
Wine Delights Journal – Book 17
Winemaking Delights Journal – Book 18

Cookbooks

Cookbook Delights Series

Apple Delights – Book 1
Blueberry Delights – Book 2
Chocolate Delights – Book 3
Grape Delights – Book 4
Huckleberry Delights – Book 5
Lentil Delights – Book 6
Onion Delights – Book 7
Peach Delights – Book 8
Pear Delights – Book 9
Plum Delights – Book 10
Prickly Pear Delights – Book 11
Pumpkin Delights – Book 12
Raspberry Delights – Book 13
Rhubarb Delights – Book 14
Strawberry Delights – Book 15
Tea Time Delights – Book 16
Wine Delights – Book 17
Winemaking Delights – Book 18

Cookbook Delights Holiday Series

New Years Delights – Book 1
Valentine Delights – Book 2
St. Patrick's Day Delights –
  Book 3
Easter Delights – Book 4
Mother's Day Delights - Book 5
Memorial Day Delights – Book 6
Father's Day Delights – Book 7
Fourth of July Delights – Book 8
Labor Day Delights – Book 9
Halloween Delights – Book 10
Thanksgiving Delights – Book 11
Christmas Delights – Book 12

Many of the above listed books are also available in bilingual and translated versions. Please contact Whispering Pine Press International, Inc., for details.

This list of books is not all-inclusive. For a complete list please visit our website or contact us at:

Whispering Pine Press International, Inc.
Your Northwest Book Publishing Company
2510 North Pines Road, Suite 206, Sales Room
Spokane Valley, WA 99206-7636 USA
Phone: (509) 928-7888 | Fax: (509) 922-9949
Email: sales@whisperingpinepress.com

Publisher Websites
Main Website: WhisperingPinePress.com
Online Store: WhisperingPinePressBookstore.com
WordPress Blogs: WhisperingPinePressBlog.com
WhisperingPinePressKidsBooks.com
WhisperingPinePressTeenBooks.com
WhisperingPinePressPoetry.com

Author Websites
Karen Jean Matsko Hood
Author Website: KarenJeanMatskoHood.com
Online Store: KarenJeanMatskoHoodBookstore.com
Author Blog: KarenJeanMatskoHoodBlog.com
Kids Books: KarensKidsBooks.com
KarensTeensBooks.com

Author's Social Media
Friend her on **Facebook**: Karen Jean Matsko Hood Author Fan Page
Please Follow the Author on **Twitter**: @KarenJeanHood
Google Plus Profile: Karen Jean Matsko Hood
Pinterest.com/KarenJMHood

About the Author and Cook

Karen Jean Matsko Hood has always enjoyed cooking, baking, and experimenting with recipes. At this time Hood is working to complete a series of cookbooks that blends her skills and experience in cooking and entertaining. Hood entertains large groups of people and especially enjoys designing creative menus with holiday, international, ethnic, and regional themes.

Hood is publishing a cookbook series entitled the *Cookbook Delights Series*, in which each cookbook emphasizes a different food ingredient or theme. The first cookbook in the series is *Apple Delights Cookbook*. Hood is working to complete another series of cookbooks titled *Hood and Matsko Family Cookbooks*, which includes many recipes handed down from her family heritage and others that have emerged from more current family traditions. She has been invited to speak on talk radio shows on various topics, and favorite recipes from her cookbooks have been prepared on local television programs.

Hood was born and raised in Great Falls, Montana. As an undergraduate, she attended the College of St. Benedict in St. Joseph, Minnesota, and St. John's University in Collegeville, Minnesota. She attended the University of Great Falls in Great Falls, Montana. Hood received a B.S. Degree in Natural Science from the College of St. Benedict and minored in both Psychology and Secondary Education. Upon her graduation, Hood and her husband taught science and math on the island of St. Croix in the U.S. Virgin Islands. Hood has completed postgraduate classes at the University of Iowa in Iowa City, Iowa. In May 2001, she completed her Master's Degree in Pastoral Ministry at Gonzaga University in Spokane, Washington. She has taken postgraduate classes at Lewis and Clark College on the North Idaho college campus in Coeur d'Alene, Idaho, Taylor University in Fort Wayne, Indiana, Spokane Falls Community College, Spokane Community College, Washington State University, University of Washington, and Eastern Washington University. Hood is working on research projects to complete her Ph.D. in Leadership Studies at Gonzaga University in Spokane, Washington.

Hood resides in Spokane, Washington, along with her husband, many of her sixteen children, and foster children. Her interests include writing, research, and teaching. She previously has volunteered as a court advocate in the Spokane juvenile court system for abused and neglected children.

Hood is a literary advocate for youth and adults. Her hobbies include cooking, baking, collecting, photography, indoor and outdoor gardening, farming, and the cultivation of unusual flowering plants and orchids.

She enjoys raising several specialty breeds of animals including Babydoll Southdown, Friesen, and Icelandic sheep, Icelandic horses, bichons frisés, cockapoos, Icelandic sheepdogs, a Newfoundland, a Rottweiler, a variety of Nubian and fainting goats, and a few rescue cats. Hood also enjoys bird-watching and finds all aspects of nature precious.

She demonstrates a passionate appreciation of the environment and a respect for all life. She also invites you to visit her websites:

www.KarenJeanMatskoHood.com www.
KarenJeanMatskoHoodBookstore.com
www.KarenJeanMatskoHoodBlog.com
www.KarensKidsBooks.com

www.HoodFamilyBlog.com
www.HoodFamily.com

Author's Social Media
Friend her on **Facebook**: Karen Jean Matsko Hood Author Fan Page
Please Follow the Author on **Twitter**: @KarenJeanHood
Google Plus Profile: Karen Jean Matsko Hood
Pinterest.com/KarenJMHood

www.ingramcontent.com/pod-product-compliance
Lightning Source LLC
Chambersburg PA
CBHW060859280326
41934CB00007B/1113